REMEMBERING A PLACE I'VE NEVER BEEN

REMEMBERING A PLACE I'VE NEVER BEEN

the past in three voices

Heather Bauchop

Cold Hub Press

First edition

Cold Hub Press
PO Box 156
Lyttelton 8841
New Zealand
coldhubpress.co.nz

ISBN: 978-0-473-45367-1

A catalogue record for this book is available
from the National Library of New Zealand

Cover image: Manse, Ollaberry, detail of
United Presbyterian church and manse, Ollaberry
(ST00230, Shetland Museum and Archive)

Author photograph: Isaac Bennett

Printed by Toltech Print Ltd, Christchurch, New Zealand

Contents

Part One: Home

Part Two: History

Part Three: Noone

To Sheila May Christian Finlayson,
the girl I never met,
and to my daughter Pippi Finlay Miller
and the woman she is becoming.

Just after this collection was submitted
to Cold Hub Press, I was awarded
a mentorship by the New Zealand Society of Authors.
I would like to thank NZSA for their support and my mentor
James Norcliffe for his lively exchanges.

To my friends and family who read
or at least took away earlier versions
of the manuscript, thank you.

To Richard and Pippi—
thanks for sharing my words and your love.

'Broadly speaking, there are two kinds of map:
the grid and the story . . .'

—Robert Macfarlane, *The Wild Places*

'Item: I leave to the future
that flaky blistered rusted
tangled tumbledown
crock of shit that is the past'

—James Norcliffe, *Villon in Millerton*

Part One: Home

A map

I've never had to navigate—
my path was paved by my father's eyes.

Now the map, unfolded
has a crease

words are lost
in the wear and tear

of moments.
There is no key for time.

So many minutes have passed.

With my finger

With my finger I trace years:
oceans, winding roads

a railway station car park
in the rain

a boy, alone
on the platform.

Narrative

Death is its own story—
a narrative from
grave to grave
a line of anguish
in cramped cursive.

Look, here are my hands
years marked by liver spots
and a fan of tendons. They empty
a jam jar of spent flowers.

My father is gone
along the path through time—
its measured steps watched over
by the stony eyes of angels.

Six feet was deep enough
to keep away the fear of plague
bury the terror of an unlived life.
Here's a wreath of wilted roses—
dance now, before death
knocks on the door.

But there is no hiding: this mortality
my only clear inheritance.

And his words with him

He has taken his silence.

Only his teeth remain
loose
in bony sockets.

But here—
a sheaf of scraps
and sayings.

I am left to stitch together
these words—
they will be my shroud.

Other deaths are far away

My father left those other stones—
with their hyphenated lives
body upon body until time collapsed
its skeleton dismantled
amongst rotten winding sheets
splintered timbers.

His was no corpse road
from church to tomb
but a series of crossroads—
no witch ball to snare the past
that chased him over grey sea—
distance entangled those relentless steps.

Now he is in the ground
I will turn, hold before me
this glass ball of threads
see the blue-lit faces
that follow me.

His name

I have only
his name.

Beneath my feet
someone else's earth—

even if I found the place
with standing stones and my name

etched in granite certainty
would that place be mine

or just the past looking ahead
with blind sight?

If I knew where I came from
could I be somewhere else?

I was brought here

Peripatetic you would call them—
my father, his father before him.

They left a trail, slick
with bloody movement

their knowing dismembered
between remote islands.

I read this place
on my body, scarify myself

with ridgelines, each line of hills
a story I cannot follow.

What does it matter when I go?

Even if I leave tomorrow
it will make no difference—

this map with its accursed creases
shows a sealed road through hills

where thought
once made its way lightly.

Word of mouth

My father said his father
came from a place

where sons were called
after their fathers.

Can there be that many
matching names?

And did they all
have to live

on the same
narrow
road?

Heritage

A stone cottage
but and ben

two rooms hazy from peat fires
and the fear of God—

or maybe a house, one
among row upon row of terraces

cobbled roads ringing
with the bicycle bells

of mill workers
in the bleary dawn.

Bequest

The North Sea where the empty wind
whips blind waves.

Look to the horizon—
a worn headland

where once a mother
farewelled her son.

The cold wind at my back
beneath a mantle of long white cloud.

Always the waves.

Evidence

On my desk the past—
justified by superscript.
See the careful advance
of punctuated moments.

The evidence:
a pile of papers
certified
registered
and yet . . .

I take out the shoebox
my father left in the drawer
of his bureau—

a photograph of bare hills
a house with empty windows

the door closed.

Fertility

The past produces a billion babies
but here I struggle for a fertile word.

Empty inheritance—
the editors shake their heads
at my strange sterility.

This body ejaculates words
but there is no one to read them—
the future an empty fluid
on my palm.

Seconds

A house at the head of the bay
the stone wall with a gate
leading to the beach.

The empty hills
call out their silence.

How can this grey sea be my blood?
The cold wind my breath?

I have never trod this peaty ground
where tales are held
in the leathery skin of time.

Give me back those storms
and the silver herring sea,
a burn with brown trout
caught on the fly
fried in oatmeal for breakfast.

I taste seconds.

Another photograph

Two boys stand at the knee of a man
whose hand is on the older boy's shoulder.

The younger leans
slightly away.

Behind
on the steps of the kirk
a girl squints into a chill sun.

Provenance

Why do people not write
on the backs of photographs—

take a moment
of pencilled
responsibility!

Are those
my mother's eyes
looking back at me?

Tight

Blue words dragged
across unlined paper, diagonals of ink

obscuring earlier writing—
saving paper.

This crabbed penny pinching
reminds me of my father

who trimmed
the edges of letters

and saved a couple of cents
by leaving out the word

love.

Progeny

Words are my only children.

What if they go astray?

Past perfect

I am too old
to father moments

gone those days
when I thought

I held the future
in my arms

and she spoke to me
in sighs.

I believed each murmur
imagining in my body

an ongoing story
when all the time

I was first person
singular.

In dreams

Thick thick walls
and a small window.

I look from the croft
to the bay and see

what the tide has left
among the shells.

But what of the wind?

But what of the wind
and the open sea
the soul landlocked
in stone-walled
gardens, the eyes
that match wintry skies?
My blood. The path
lost in the intricate
breeze that teases
the clifftop grass—
a woman considering
the gathering clouds
before leaping.

Proof

How could I know the feeling of air
against outstretched arms

the embrace of broken rocks wreathed
in welcoming foam?

It is here—on paper
stamped, signed, dated.

She will not be in the churchyard
but is banished, like me

to the enclosing earth
beyond the crossroads

followed by the swinging
lanterns of mourners

outside the sanctity
of the drystone walls.

Mourning

The wake recedes.

There is a rhythm to this mourning
a pitch and roll, as the gull's wings
dip in the turbulent air
and the past pulls away.

Home.

All that's left—
the sun rising
on this treeless landscape
drawn with my eyes closed.

Grave

What covers her
is not rich soil

but words formed
by my empty mouth.

Now the words are said
there is nothing left to bury.

Travails

Even as I see myself
sitting by the wall

I cannot cross.

My father took from me
this place

yet here I am.

This land

This land beneath my feet
This land under my nails

This land will bury me.

Part Two: History

In residence

Stone. Two storey.
Aspirations.
Bluestone quarried locally—see the scar
on the hill behind the trees.

Limestone-faced windows, doors and quoins
the roof, slate (Welsh: I have an account)
original window joinery
internal layout largely unchanged.

The servant's call system—the annunciator—
still works: a row of bells by the rear stairs
sprung on coiled steel, a corresponding pull
to the left of each fireplace.

Much of the interior fabric
dates from the late nineteenth
or early twentieth century.
The fireplaces are original.

I can feel the cold coming up through the floor.
Look: rising damp in the corner of the bay window
in what would have been the withdrawing room
suggests underfloor ventilation or drainage problems.

Mr Noone says his father
had a plumber look at it years ago.
I don't think the young man in overalls
outside the window is old enough to drive

let alone conceptualise the drainage scheme
of a gentleman farmer's residence
completed in 1882 (the date
inscribed in stone at the gable peak).

Inheritance

She grew up in town
in a new subdivision—
bungalows with jaunty
porches and all the mod cons.

She met him when
he came to town for Show Day
all those years ago.
This is the family farm.

She married the eldest son.
In every stone he sees his father
alone in the house all those years
after his mother died.

She sees her own grave. Their sons
don't want an old house with a dairy factory
in the view shaft and effluent ponds
just behind that stand of remnant bush

and the daughter only comes
to see them on Sundays
to check
if they're still alive.

Technological assistance

To identify the architect of the house
using the digitized

collection of nineteenth
century newspapers

enter the search terms
architect, tender, erection.

Here is something
I could use.

Details

The article in the *Witness* gives
a detailed description of each room:

the grandeur of the hallway
the use of rare timbers in the ballroom
the panelled smoking room to which
the gentlemen retire after dinner.

Did they discuss the price of the marble mantelpieces
the quality of the ornate cast plaster ceiling
or admire the image of the Kent countryside painted in oils
by his late wife on the panels of the dining room door?

The *Witness* reports his wife wore a dove grey dress
trimmed with Brussels lace and performed Schumann
on the pianoforte and that the Misses Smythe
were visiting from Sydney before returning Home.

How delicious standing at the window
watching the ladies making eyes at their corseted futures
covering their mouths with gloved hands
as they curve their lips.

Rooms

In the morning the maid of all work
throws open the heavy curtains
and unlatches the windows
picks up the cigar bands
and clears the brandy balloons
from the occasional table.

But this is supposition: there are no accounts
of the woman on her knees at the grate
just the presence of an unheated room
under the attic roof reached by a narrow stair
shown on the architectural drawings
and labelled 'maid's room'.

Plans

The hand-inked lines, careful watercolour
revealing the construction materials

the architect's signature
in the bottom right corner

and the contractor's mark
and date, on the left: a perfect concept.

I'm left with the house:
the owner's intrusive alterations—

the ugly compartments
of change and time.

Key

'*Stone*—yellow ochre, sepia, burnt umber; if for sections,
the tints or shades of those should be darker than those
used for the elevations.
Brick, ordinary kind—Lake, mixed with a little light red or burnt sienna;
for brick in section, a deeper shade.
Concrete—sepia with dots, short dashes, or markings of a deeper shade.
Wood—yellow ochre, with short dashes of a deeper tint.
Cast iron—Indigo, with a little Indian ink; in section, a
deeper tint.
Lead—Indian ink, very pale, with short dashes of pale indigo.
Slate—A mixture of indigo and lake.
Tiles—Red.
Plaster—Lines of a pale blue'[1]

[1] "The Finishing of Drawings", *Technical Drawing and Design for Students of Architecture and Building*, (London and Glasgow: William Collins, Sons, and Co., 1875), Chapter 5, Part 2, 22–24; cited in Jane E. Sugarman, "Observations on the Materials and Techniques Used in 19th Century American Architectural Presentation Drawings", *Book and Paper Group Annual*, Volume 05, 1986, The American Institute for Conservation.

Evidence

See, in the corner
of the built-in wardrobe
where the painter
thought nobody
would notice
there is a remnant
of wallpaper—
blocked colour
Scheele's green
botanical motifs
a repeating pattern.

Through our skin
and with each breath
we take in that old poison.

Oh, but it is beautiful.

Camping

It's just the two of them: in the winter
they must shut themselves in what was
the original kitchen and draw straws to decide
who will turn on the electric blankets.

I'd camp by the fire
that monstrosity she insisted he install
having survived the first winter
when the bread froze on the table.

He is waiting

The daughter insists he go into a Home.
She tells me his new room
has a pleasant outlook: he will be warm.

He sits in the window of the withdrawing room
his death in the air like the rising damp
the plumber is still considering.

His wife brings tea, the bone china cups
rattle on their saucers.

They sit opposite me
a table between them, cups set aside.
He has crumbs on his chin.
She will not speak—it is not her story.

He waits for words
one eye on the past
while the other already
sees the future.

Home

'This is my home.'

He is saying goodbye.
Home is already a place
he is seeing in retrospect.
The new home a confinement
where family will visit—
which he will never leave.

For those who came before him
home was also a place
to which they could not return
banished as they were by distance.

Dispossessed of time and place
I see their world: the dark trees
the house, words speaking
through the stones—the words
I read as the days draw in.

Fact checking

Is there pit-sawn timber in that structure
in the trees behind the homestead?

Are those cut nails?

What's under the roofing iron?

Does the iron have a maker's mark?

That reference on page 23.

Do all the astragals on the dormer windows
have that same lamb's tongue profile?

Is there really a grave?

What was the purpose of the white room out the back?

In that final family photograph, the last one taken
before his grandfather died, is that *Wellingtonia* planted?
The tree should be visible in the background,
past the veranda post on which the old man leans.

Legend has it

There was a fire that's why there are no records.

He married a Maori princess.

He was a remittance man.

My grandmother remembers.

When I was a boy.

It's always been like that.

It says so here.

Unplanned

Square, stone-walled with a high window.
Access through a narrow passage
and up three stairs. The door is heavy
and has a slide bolt lock.
No handle on the inside.

There is no piped water supply.
Electrical wiring has never
been extended to this room.
It holds its temperature well:
a solid cell guarding the contents of its history.

Why is this room not shown on the plans?

Intrusive investigations

Here a loose board—
an opportunity to investigate the foundations
and establish the structural details of this odd room.

All manner of objects turn up under the floors
and in the walls of dwellings—dead cats, boots and shoes.

Bent pins and candle writing, scribbled
eyes that challenge the wrath of an angry God,
these conceal intentional forgetting and considered remembering—
a cache to safeguard the future.

Here is fear
on the subfloor of the heart.

At the tips of my fingers
covered in dust, a fountain pen—
a scratching of apotropaic marks
call forth the virgin past.

Off limits

'We never really
used that room,' she says.

He chews his words and spits out:
'Father's storeroom, I used to run past it

when I went to see Maude in the kitchen
when she promised me sweeties.

When he died I unlocked the door.
The room was empty.'

View shaft

Through the high square
of the single window—

trees bow in penitence:
like me they are strangers

toppled by storms, clinging
by their shallow roots

to this new land.

Past the trees

There is a fenced area
and a fallen stone.

The house has turned its back.
Who lies behind?

Holes

On the fallen stone
the lead lettering of 'died'
stands proud

the rest of the story
has dropped out
leaving only the peg holes of memory.

Buried discontinuities

Survey a matrix, converting time
into distance at measurable velocities.

On the screen the vertical shaft
and the hyperbolic reflection of past lives:

Two graves: both adult, one shown only
by the vertical disturbance and discontinuity

compared to the surrounding subsoil—
the other a stack of echoes, lead-lined containment

a casket to stave off
the threat of time.

Recommendations

For the conservation of this place
bound and peer-reviewed
here is a checklist for the future:

- Time is to be altered
  in like materials
- Any written changes
  to history will be shown
  [in square brackets]

Signed _______________

Dated_______________

Reviewer_____________

Part Three: Noone

Title proper: Notebook
General material: Textual Records
Level of description: File
Repository: Archives and Special Collections
Reference Code: ASC N 1982-nd-001

Physical description: 0.5cm of textual records

Name of Creator: Noone family papers
Scope and content: The file contains a personal notebook. Author not identified. Undated
Name access point: Noone

Cast

Him sitting on that ladder-back chair
looking out of the frame. Her

hand on his shoulder.
Her eyes accuse me—

but how can she know that
wall-eyed, here

I am the future?

Debt

Blood-smeared gaze
to the left ear of my father.

He turns to look over his shoulder
leaving Maude

to put coins
on my mother's eyes.

In plain sight

He covers my wandering eye

but oh I see him
I see him.

He thinks I cannot know myself

he forgets
I see myself in his eyes.

Seeing

My hair cut so if I pull a lock past my ear
it is not my eyes that tell me the colour

but my fingers as they twitch
the hair out by the root—

the strand I hold to the light
is silver, like morning.

He must be sad
that I bring new days

while he carries the night
in a storm that frames his face.

She tells me

'So beautiful, your mother,' says Maude
'if you could have only seen her.'

I know I am a poor replacement for beauty—
I see that with my other eye

within the words
she does not say about me.

So why do they keep me?

I lived.

Concealment

In this room built of cut stone
surrounded by charred stumps

white in this dark place
he keeps his grief.

Through the window I see how he has placed
the shaped stones of forgetting

bounded by the post and rail fence
confining memory.

He replaced her

She was barely cold, Maude's fingers still aching
from the tiny stitches that make up the work of death
but he turned his eyes to that girl
and she was but a girl

in this land where men are as common as sheep—
a girl by her father's knee. She would provide
for a lusty future, sons to break the land
with their commanding voices

but here, in this white room
I am what she doesn't yet know
she should fear.

Words

There was a time when the past
rocked like a cradle, back and forth
the arc of many days.

Maude tells me it was she who rocked me
until cradle became bed and time
made me taller than the dresser.

Maude gave me my words
they spilled from her lips
and with her finger she shaped each letter.

The dark water on white stone sluiced away
silence and so she gave me my voice.
Maude stands in the doorway

eyes to the floor, hands clasped
in front of her apron. He does not know
which eye to watch.

Maude sees my words waiting.
She stands back to let him through
and locks the door behind him.

Later, a shuffle under the door:
a notebook; later still, concealed
beneath the cloth covering

my now-empty piss pot
pen and ink
and a hot stream of words.

Seeing double

When I was small I would catch him
looking, I would say

stealing a glance—it was not the eye
that I would have given him.

'Look at me when I talk to you,' he'd say.

Oh, I can see. I see what you are carrying

on your shoulders—I bring
what you would leave behind.

She never comes here

Maude says that the girl
a woman now of course
sits in the drawing room.
She has a straight back
and small feet, her hair
is a tumble of curls
her teeth are pearls.

The neighbouring wives
and daughters pay their calls
hiding their ruined hands
and their grubby petticoats,
dragged through the ruts
by goaty husbands.

Maude comes to that insistent ring
of servitude that even now I hear.
She looks at the door
and leaves me my bread.

My window

This window is as wide and as deep
as two courses of stone. I have counted each stone
for as many years as I have known numbers.

Under the loose board, I scratch each day:
it is here that time is hidden.

Outside, I can see the edge of the sweeping drive.
Beyond the black trees that lean over the fence
Maude points out my mother's grave.

Time

Time is grooves
cut in the corner of the day.

Time is a nail pried loose
from the still life of trees

cut in bored lengths
wide as the dark.

I hold this auger
in my hand.

There is no secret. I know
what it foretells.

In my hands

Maude gives me my years
a finger at a time.

I remember when I had a whole decade
in my closed fists. When I ran out of fingers

she let me have her hand
to hold in mine.

Her hands

Her hands tell their own red and callous time.

But here, a soft moment
on the inside of her wrist.

I meet her eye

When I clung to her knees
my face buried in her skirts

Maude would place her hand on my hair
before she left and locked the door.

Now when I cling to her
I see the pulse in her neck.

Her fingers beneath my chin, she lifts my face
and puts her lips to my other eye.

My days

Light is brought in a bowl.
I hold its heat between my hands
and drink the days that follow

one after another.
Light is as sharp as the knife Maude brings—
a bright edge that cuts time into seasons.

Light is blunt and heavy
as it clubs the dying day
and drags it behind the hills.

Spare

'I only have a moment to spare,'
Maude says. I could give her mine.

I can neither discard the passing moments
nor remove the minutes as they crowd before me.

A mound

There behind those distant trees
the stone mother, the one Maude gave me
is not alone.
                    Beside her a mound
and a woman drawn tight in black thoughts
standing as alone as all my nights.

Age

Maude saw me watching:
'She was your age when she came here.'

Her time is stillborn
but now, see how she mourns moments.

Confined

There’s no one to see
as I stand at the window.

Maude comes in with my bread.
A man mounts his horse.

‘That’s the doctor,’ Maude says.
‘She’s confined.’

I count months on my fingers.
But there she is again

alone by the trees.

Avert

One morning I saw the silhouettes
of small crosses

against the early light, and the kneeling figure
with hands clasped.

She turned
and caught my other eye.

Unlaced

I knew she would come.

Hers is not a sound I have heard before—
this tentative opening, the crack in the door
the curl of a small hand, her breath
held and then, it is all of her—
see the pinched waist
and the glance of that stockinged ankle.
A curl has fallen from her bun
her eyes are violent
and she is pouting those generous lips
the swollen lower one
caught between pearly teeth.

'So,' she says, 'you are here.'

She comes back and back

I didn't know life had so many moments—
mine being marked by so few.

Yet here is the door
sidling open

her commanding eyes shining
in the light of morning.

How tight, those stays

She does not know
whether to look
at my other eye.

But my queer eye
for all its squint
sees what she wants.

Shifting moments

She looks at my flesh
white as stone.

She will stay with me
if he ever finds her here.

And yet she does not move
when I undo her bodice, release her stays

or as her skirt falls away
leaving petticoats

and the light shift
of moments.

Her voice is mine

Maude had showed me, that place
where soft eyes see only the gentle parting.

Yes, my words are on her lips.
Oh! how beautifully she says them

full of pregnant pauses and lament.
We are children of our time

me the past
and she the swollen future.

Hear how time
cries out for us.

Hear it.

Later she is heavy

She comes, her hand pressed
to the small of her back.

She has forsaken
the corseted future.

In split petticoats, she leans
on my chaste iron bed frame.

My fingers tell me
her time is near.

What I hear

Though I am walled in stone
and have but a solitary window

the air around me
is wrenched with her screams.

The birds in the dark trees take flight
even as the light fades.

It is the silence

Maude's mouth is sealed.
A line across her face

and her eyes on the floor.
It has been days.

She has swallowed her words.
I hope they burn in her throat.

In my arms

Maude stands by the door.
In her arms a swaddled infant
held to her breast.

She places him in my arms.

A cradle

I sit in the corner of the room.
My hand rocks the cradle.

I hear the thin wail of time passing.
I hold that unsteady gaze

find myself looking over my left shoulder
back into the future.

Forgetting

I will put away my book and pen:
the future is no longer mine

but is carried in these squint eyes
looking at me now and then.

This is the deal I make with time
to allow me to remember.

Recall

His eye follows
as I hold up my finger

the finger for this first day.
This is my gift—time.

And I whisper the words Maude gave to me—
'So beautiful your mother.'

One day, in his square window
when he has run out of hands

and no longer has mine to hold
he will write on white stone

and perhaps recall my face.